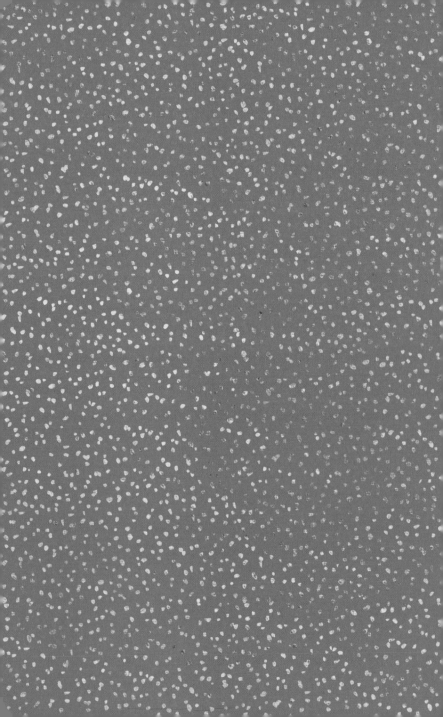

THIS BOOK BELONGS TO

....

Congratulations,
GRADUATE!

Ellie Claire® Gift & Paper Expressions
Franklin, TN 37067
EllieClaire.com
Ellie Claire is a registered trademark of Worthy Media, Inc.

Congratulations, Graduate
© 2017 by Ellie Claire
Published by Ellie Claire, an imprint of Worthy Publishing Group,
a division of Worthy Media, Inc.

ISBN 9781633261792

Stock or custom editions of Ellie Claire titles may be purchased in bulk
for educational, business, ministry, fundraising, or sales promotional use.
For information, please e-mail info@EllieClaire.com

Excluding Scripture verses, references to men and masculine pronouns have
been replaced with gender-neutral references.

Cover and interior design by Jeff Jansen | AestheticSoup.net

Printed in China

1 2 3 4 5 6 7 8 9 RRD 22 21 20 19 18 17

CONTENTS

Way to Go!

···

The tassel's
worth the hassle!

$\mathcal{Y}$ou have brains in your head.
You have feet in your shoes.
You can steer yourself in
any direction you choose.
You're on your own.
And you know what you know.
You are the one
who'll decide where to go....
Just never forget
to be dexterous and deft
And never mix up
your right foot with your left.

DR. SEUSS

$\mathcal{A}$ graduation ceremony is an event
where the commencement speaker tells thousands
of students dressed in identical caps and gowns
that "individuality" is the key to success.

ROBERT ORBEN

$\mathcal{W}$hen you leave here, don't forget why you came.

ADLAI STEVENSON

Keep company with GOD,
get in on the best.
Open up before GOD, keep nothing back;
He'll do whatever needs to be done:
He'll validate your life in the clear light of day.

PSALM 37:4-6 MSG

No pessimist ever discovered the secrets
of the stars, or sailed to an uncharted land,
or opened a new heaven to the human spirit.

HELEN KELLER

Achievement is the knowledge that you have
studied and worked hard and done the best that is in you.
Success is being praised by others, and that's nice,
too, but not as important or satisfying.
Always aim for achievement and forget about success.

HELEN HAYES

$\mathcal{A}$t commencement you wear your square-shaped
mortarboards. My hope is that from time to time
you will let your minds be bold, and wear sombreros.

PAUL FREUND

$\mathcal{A}$ span of life is nothing. But the man or woman
who lives that span, they are something. They can fill
that tiny span with meaning, so its quality is immeasurable,
though its quantity may be insignificant.

CHAIM POTOK

$\mathcal{S}$ome succeed because they are destined to,
but most succeed because they are determined to.

His master praised him for good work. "You have been faithful in handling this small amount," he told him, "so now I will give you many more responsibilities. Begin the joyous tasks I have assigned to you."

MATTHEW 25:21 TLB

The reward for work well done
is the opportunity to do more.

To those of you who received honors,
awards, and distinctions, I say,
"Well done." And to the "C" students, I say,
"You, too, may one day be President of the United States."

GEORGE W. BUSH

There's no thrill in easy sailing
when the skies are clear and blue,
There's no joy in merely doing things
which anyone can do.
But there is some satisfaction
that is mighty sweet to take,
when you reach a destination
that you thought you'd never make.

Not because we think we can do anything of lasting value
by ourselves. Our only power and success comes from God.
2 CORINTHIANS 3:5 TLB

No matter what your age or your situation,
your dreams are achievable. Whether you're five or 105,
you have a lifetime ahead of you!

New Beginnings

....

Each day can be the beginning
of a wonderful future.

What we feel, think, and do this moment
influences both our present and the future in ways
we may never know. Begin. Start right where you are.
Consider your possibilities and find inspiration...
to add more meaning and zest to your life.

ALEXANDRA STODDARD

Graduation is a time of completion, of finishing,
of an ending; however, it is also a time of celebration
of achievement and a beginning for the new graduate.

CATHERINE PULSIFER

The LORD's lovingkindnesses indeed never cease,
For His compassions never fail;
They are new every morning;
Great is Your faithfulness.

LAMENTATIONS 3:22–23 NASB

This bright, new day, complete with 24 hours of opportunities, choices, and attitudes, comes with a perfectly matched set of 1,440 minutes. This unique gift, this one day, cannot be exchanged, replaced, or refunded. Handle with care. Make the most of it. There is only one to a customer!

There will come a time when you believe everything is finished. That will be the beginning.

LOUIS L'AMOUR

Begin today! No matter how feeble the light, let it shine as best it may. The world may need just that quality of light which you have.

HENRY C. BLINN

What we call the end is also a beginning.
The end is where we start from.

T. S. ELIOT

Today is unique! It has never occurred before
and it will never be repeated. At midnight it will end,
quietly, suddenly, totally. Forever. But the hours between
now and then are opportunities with eternal possibilities.

CHARLES R. SWINDOLL

This is the day the LORD has made;
We will rejoice and be glad in it.

PSALM 118:24 NKJV

*E*ach of my days are miracles.
I won't waste my day; I won't throw away a miracle.

KELLEY VICKSTROM

*E*ach morning is a fresh beginning. Each day the world
is made new. Today is your new day when your world
is made new. You have lived all your life up to this
moment to come to this day. This moment, this day,
is as good as any moment in all eternity. Try to make
of this day—each moment of this day—a heaven on earth.
This is your day of opportunity.

*L*ive your life while you have it.
Life is a splendid gift—there is nothing small about it.

FLORENCE NIGHTINGALE

I like living. I have sometimes been wildly,
despairingly, acutely miserable, racked with sorrow,
but through it all I still know quite certainly
that just to be alive is a grand thing.

AGATHA CHRISTIE

We may run, walk, stumble, drive, or fly,
but let us never lose sight of the reason for the journey,
or miss a chance to see a rainbow on the way.

GLORIA GAITHER

Wisdom is sweet to your soul;
if you find it, there is a future hope for you,
and your hope will not be cut off.

PROVERBS 24:14 NIV

Life Is a School

....

Life is a school. There is something
new to learn wherever we may be,
wherever we go, wherever we turn.

WALTER A. WITT

It is important that you realize that you are not a finished
product. You are still in the process of creation.
In fact, all of us are in the process of creation....
But we do have a divine heritage and we are here
for noble purposes. We have an infinitely important future
potential, if we learn. How is it going to happen?
Will it be automatic? You who are married,
did the ceremony create you or qualify you as properly
equipped husbands and wives? Does the birth of a baby
into the family qualify you as adequate parents?
Does graduation signify that we are educated?

MARION D. HANKS

You have made known to me the path of life;
you will fill me with joy in Your presence,
with eternal pleasures at Your right hand.

PSALM 16:11 NIV

*A*nyone who stops learning is old, whether at twenty or eighty. Anyone who keeps learning stays young.

HENRY FORD

*I*t is indeed ironic that we spend our school days yearning to graduate and our remaining days waxing nostalgic about our school days.

ISABEL WAXMAN

*E*ducation is a lifelong process of which schooling is only a small but necessary part. As long as one remains alive and healthy, learning can go on—and should.

MORTIMER J. ADLER

*S*how me Your ways, O Lord;
Teach me Your paths.
Lead me in Your truth and teach me.

PSALM 25:4-5 NKJV

The trouble with learning from experience
is that you never graduate.

DOUG LARSON

Let us think of education as the means of developing our
greatest abilities, because in each of us there is a private
hope and dream which, fulfilled, can be translated into
benefit for everyone and greater strength for our nation.

JOHN F. KENNEDY

Your schooling may be over, but remember
that your education still continues.

All of the top achievers I know are lifelong learners...
looking for new skills, insights, and ideas.
If they're not learning, they're not growing...
not moving toward excellence.

DENIS WAITLEY

I have learned that success is to be measured
not so much by the position that one has reached
in life as by the obstacles which one has overcome
while trying to succeed.

BOOKER T. WASHINGTON

The person who graduates today and stops learning
tomorrow is uneducated the day after.

NEWTON D. BAKER

Is life not full of opportunities for learning love?
Every man and woman every day has a thousand of them.
The world is not a playground, it is a schoolroom.
Life is not a holiday, but an education. And the one
eternal lesson for us all is how better we can love.

HENRY DRUMMOND

*L*ife is my college. May I graduate well,
and earn some honors!
LOUISA MAY ALCOTT

*G*od sets out the entire creation as a science classroom,
using birds and beasts to teach wisdom.
JOB 35:11 MSG

*G*od shall be my hope, my stay,
my guide and lantern to my feet.
WILLIAM SHAKESPEARE

Designs on Your Future

May God's love guide you through
the special plans He has for your life.

*L*ive for today but hold your hands open to tomorrow.
Anticipate the future and its changes with joy.
There is a seed of God's love in every event, every
circumstance, every unpleasant situation in which
you may find yourself.... Allow your dreams a place
in your prayers and plans. God-given dreams can help
you move into the future He is preparing for you.

BARBARA JOHNSON

I'll take the hand of those who don't know the way,
who can't see where they're going.
I'll be a personal guide to them,
directing them through unknown country.

ISAIAH 42:16 MSG

*T*hose who build the future are those who know
that greater things are yet to come, and that they
themselves will help bring them about.

MELVIN J. EVANS

The patterns of our days are always changing…
rearranging…and each design for living is unique…
graced with its own special beauty.

Joy comes from knowing God loves me
and knows who I am and where I'm going…
that my future is secure as I rest in Him.

JAMES DOBSON

You can never change the past. But by the grace of God,
you can win the future. So remember those things
which will help you forward, but forget those things
which will only hold you back.

RICHARD C. WOODSOME

Not that I have already attained,
or am already perfected; but I press on,
that I may lay hold of that for which
Christ Jesus has also laid hold of me.

PHILIPPIANS 3:12 NKJV

*N*ever be afraid to trust an unknown future
to an all-knowing God.
CORRIE TEN BOOM

It is only a tiny rosebud—
A flower of God's design;
But I cannot unfold the petals
With these clumsy hands of mine.

For the pathway that lies before me
My heavenly Father knows—
I'll trust Him to unfold the moments
Just as He unfolds the rose.

God has designs on our future…and He has designed
us for the future. He has given us something
to do in the future that no one else can do.

RUTH SENTER

Faith makes the uplook good, the outlook bright,
the inlook favorable, and the future glorious.

V. RAYMOND EDMAN

We do not understand the intricate pattern
of the stars in their courses, but we know that He who
created them does, and that just as surely as He guides
them, He is charting a safe course for us.

BILLY GRAHAM

The uncertainties of the present always give way to the enchanted possibilities of the future.

GELSEY KIRKLAND

Those who insist upon seeing with perfect clearness before they decide, never decide.

HENRI FRÉDÉRIC AMIEL

For I know the plans I have for you," declares the LORD,
"plans to prosper you and not to harm you,
plans to give you hope and a future."

JEREMIAH 29:11 NIV

The Work in Front of You

....

Everything comes to him
who hustles while he waits.

THOMAS A. EDISON

There is no hiding from work in one form or another.
Under the great sky of our endeavors we live our lives,
growing, we hope, through its seasons toward some kind
of greater perspective. Any perspective is dearly won.
Maturity and energy in our work is not granted freely
to human beings but must be adventured and discovered,
cultivated and earned. It is the result of application,
dedication, an indispensable sense of humor, and above all
a never-ending courageous conversation with ourselves,
those with whom we work, and those whom we serve.
It is a long journey, it calls on both the ardors of youth
and the perspectives of a longer view.
It is achieved through a lifelong pilgrimage.

DAVID WHYTE

Commit to the LORD whatever you do,
and your plans will succeed.

PROVERBS 16:3 NIV

*G*reat achievements begin with small opportunities.

*T*he work in front of you is God's work and not yours.
If God wants it to succeed, it will.
If God doesn't, it won't.
What God wants of you is to try!
So have courage—and move.

IGNATIUS OF LOYOLA

*G*od's training is for right now, not for some mist-shrouded
future. His purpose is for this minute, not for something
better down the road. His power and His presence
are available to you as you draw your next breath,
not for some great impending struggle. This moment
is the future for which you've been preparing!

JONI EARECKSON TADA

Work willingly at whatever you do, as though you were working for the Lord rather than for people.

COLOSSIANS 3:23 NLT

Lord...give me the gift of faith to be renewed and shared with others each day. Teach me to live this moment only, looking neither to the past with regret, nor the future with apprehension. Let love be my aim and my life a prayer.

ROSEANN ALEXANDER-ISHAM

In the business world, everyone is paid in two coins: cash and experience. Take the experience first; the cash will come later.

HAROLD GENEEN

I studied the lives of great men and famous women, and I found that the men and women who got to the top were those who did the jobs they had in hand with everything they had of energy and enthusiasm and hard work.

HARRY S TRUMAN

I long to accomplish a great and noble task, but it is my chief duty to accomplish humble tasks as though they were great and noble. The world is moved along, not only by the mighty shoves of its heroes, but also by the aggregate of the tiny pushes of each honest worker.

HELEN KELLER

$\mathcal{L}$et the favor of the Lord our God be upon us;
And confirm for us the work of our hands;
Yes, confirm the work of our hands.

PSALM 90:17 NASB

$\mathcal{I}$ don't dream of wealth and success for you.
But instead, a job you like,
skills you can perfect,
enthusiasm to lighten your heart,
friends, and love in abundance.

PAM BROWN

What Is Success?

The secret of success in life is...to be ready
for our opportunity when it comes.

BENJAMIN DISRAELI

What constitutes success? They have achieved success who have lived well; laughed often and loved much; who have gained the respect of intelligent people and the love of little children; who have filled their niche and accomplished their task; who have left the world better than they found it, whether by an improved poppy, a perfect poem, or a rescued soul; who have never lacked appreciation of earth's beauty, or failed to express it; who have always looked for the best in others and given the best they had; whose life was an inspiration; whose memory a benediction.

BESSIE ANDERSON STANLEY

Be strong and courageous, do not be afraid...
for the LORD your God is the one who goes with you.
He will not fail you or forsake you.

DEUTERONOMY 31:6 NASB

*E*nthusiasm is the element of success in everything.
It is the light that leads and the strength that lifts people
on and up in the great struggles of scientific pursuits
and of professional labor. It robs endurance of difficulty,
and makes duty a pleasure.

W. C. DOANE

*S*uccess is failure turned inside out,
The silver tint of the clouds of doubt,
And you never can tell how close you are,
It may be near when it seems so far.
So stick to the fight when you're hardest hit,
It's when things seem worst,
That you must not quit.

$\mathcal{N}$ot one word of all the good words which
the LORD your God spoke concerning you has failed;
all have been fulfilled for you, not one of them has failed.

JOSHUA 23:14 NASB

$\mathcal{T}$o dream anything that you want to dream.
That is the beauty of the human mind.
To do anything that you want to do.
That is the strength of the human will.
To trust yourself to test your limits.
That is the courage to succeed.

BERNARD EDMONDS

You've failed many times, although you may not remember. You fell down the first time you tried to walk. You nearly drowned the first time you tried to swim, didn't you? Did you hit the ball the first time you swung a bat? Heavy hitters, the ones who hit the most home runs, also strike out a lot. R. H. Macy failed seven times before his store in New York caught on. English novelist John Creasey received 753 rejection slips before he published 564 books. Babe Ruth struck out 1,330 times, but he also hit 715 home runs. Don't worry about failure. Worry about the chances you miss when you don't even try. You don't need to have the lead if you have the courage to come from behind.

$\mathcal{F}$ailure is only the opportunity
to begin again more intelligently.

HENRY FORD

$\mathcal{G}$od...rekindles burned-out lives with fresh hope,
Restoring dignity and respect to their lives—
a place in the sun!

1 SAMUEL 2:7-8 MSG

The Rewards
of Excellence

Destiny is not a matter of chance,
it is a matter of choice. It is not a thing
to be waited for; it is a thing to be achieved.

WILLIAM JENNINGS BRYAN

The most important moral of all is that excellence is where you find it. I would extend this generalization to cover not just higher education but all education from vocational high school to graduate school. We must learn to honor excellence, indeed to demand it in every socially accepted human activity, however humble that activity, and to scorn shoddiness, however exalted the activity. An excellent plumber is infinitely more admirable than an incompetent philosopher. The society which scorns excellence in plumbing because plumbing is a humble activity and tolerates shoddiness in philosophy because philosophy is an exalted activity will have neither good plumbing nor good philosophy. Neither its pipes nor its theories will hold water.

JOHN W. GARDNER

I pray that the eyes of your heart may be enlightened,
so that you will know what is the hope of His calling,
what are the riches of the glory of His inheritance
in the saints, and what is the surpassing greatness
of His power toward us who believe.

EPHESIANS 1:18-19 NASB

Every job is a self-portrait of the person who did it.
Autograph your work with excellence.

The price of success is hard work,
dedication to the job at hand, and the determination
that whether we win or lose, we have applied the best
of ourselves to the task at hand.... The quality of a person's
life is in direct proportion to their commitment
to excellence, regardless of their chosen field of endeavor.

VINCENT T. LOMBARDI

There is no road to success
but through a clear, strong purpose.

The LORD doesn't see things the way you see them.
People judge by outward appearance,
but the LORD looks at the heart.

1 SAMUEL 16:7 NLT

Going far beyond the call of duty, doing more than others
expect...is what excellence is all about. And it comes from
striving, maintaining the highest standards, looking after
the smallest detail, and going the extra mile. Excellence
means doing your very best. In everything. In every way.

The secret of joy in work is contained in one word—
excellence. To know how to do something well is to enjoy it.

If you ask God to lead you in serving Him
with your business, job, or career,
you'll be successful beyond your wildest dreams.
But to do this, you must devote your capital,
your profits, your resources, and your time to a cause
that has been given to you by God. Then look out,
because God will help you so you can devote even more
of your capital, profit, and time to His purposes.

The LORD has done great things for us,
and we are filled with joy.

PSALM 126:3 NIV

Go beyond their expectations.
Go out there and do something astonishing.

Lead the Way

A leader is an ordinary
person with extraordinary
vision and determination.

The things that haven't been done before,
Those are the things to try;
Columbus dreamed of an unknown shore
At the rim of the far-flung sky....

A few strike out, without map or chart,
Where never a man has been,
From the beaten paths they draw apart
To see what no man has seen.

There are deeds they hunger alone to do;
Though battered and bruised and sore,
They blaze the path for the many, who
Do nothing not done before.

The things that haven't been done before
Are the tasks worth while today;
Are you one of the flock that follows, or
Are you one that shall lead the way?

EDGAR A. GUEST

The measure of leadership is the caliber of people
who choose to follow you.

DENNIS A. PEER

One of the best ways to persuade others
is with your ears—by listening to them.

DEAN RUSK

Trust in the LORD with all your heart,
And lean not on your own understanding;
In all your ways acknowledge Him,
And He shall direct your paths.

PROVERBS 3:5-6 NKJV

Example is not the main thing in influencing others.
It is the only thing.

ALBERT SCHWEITZER

*L*eadership is not a one-day thing. It is a constant
commitment to excellence, a habit…a daily practice.

A good leader inspires others to have confidence
in people; a great leader inspires them
to have confidence in themselves.

A leader is one who knows the way,
goes the way, and shows the way.
JOHN C. MAXWELL

*H*e who chooses the beginning of a road
chooses the place it leads to.
It is the means that determine the end.
HARRY EMERSON FOSDICK

To lead people walk behind them.

Surely goodness and mercy shall follow me
All the days of my life;
And I will dwell in the house of the LORD
Forever.

PSALM 23:6 NKJV

Management is doing things right;
leadership is doing the right things.

PETER F. DRUCKER

Don't follow the path. Go where there is no path
and begin the trail. When you start a new trail
equipped with courage, strength, and conviction,
the only thing that can stop you is you!

RUBY BRIDGES

Leadership should be born out of the understanding
of the needs of those who would be affected by it.

MARIAN ANDERSON

If your actions inspire others to dream more, learn more,
do more, and become more, you are a leader.

JOHN QUINCY ADAMS

The best leader is the one who has sense enough to pick
good people to do what needs to be done, and self-restraint
enough to keep from meddling with them while they do it.

Whoever wants to be a leader
among you must be your servant.

MARK 10:43 NLT

The Value of Character

....

What really matters
is what happens in us, not to us.

D. JAMES KENNEDY

Twelve things to remember—
(1) The value of time.
(2) The success of perseverance.
(3) The pleasure of working.
(4) The dignity of simplicity.
(5) The worth of character.
(6) The power of kindness.
(7) The influence of example.
(8) The obligation of duty.
(9) The wisdom of economy.
(10) The virtue of patience.
(11) The improvement of talent.
(12) The joy of origination.

MARSHALL FIELD

Nothing is easier than saying words.
Nothing is harder than living them, day after day.
What you promise today must be renewed and redecided
tomorrow and each day that stretches out before you.

ARTHUR GORDON

Then Jesus again spoke to them,
saying, "I am the Light of the world;
he who follows Me will not walk in the darkness,
but will have the Light of life."

JOHN 8:12 NASB

Reputation is what folks think you are. Personality is what
you seem to be. Character is what you really are.

ALFRED ARMAND MONTAPERT

Doing is usually connected with a vocation or a career,
how we make a living. Being is much deeper. It relates
to character, who we are, and how we make a life.

CHARLES R. SWINDOLL

What you do when you don't have to determines
what you will be when you can no longer help it.

RUDYARD KIPLING

I am not bound to win, but I am bound to be true:
I am not bound to succeed,
but I am bound to live up to what light I have.

ABRAHAM LINCOLN

The measure of a person's real character is what they
would do if they knew they never would be found out.

THOMAS MACAULAY

You *are* right and You *do* right, God;
Your decisions are right on target.
You rightly instruct us in how to live
ever faithful to You.

PSALM 119:137 MSG

We must use time creatively, and forever realize
that the time is always right to do what is right.

MARTIN LUTHER KING JR.

What people actually need is not a tensionless state
but rather the striving and struggling for some
goal worthy of them. What they need is not
the discharge of tension at any cost, but the call
of a potential meaning waiting to be fulfilled by them.

VIKTOR FRANKL

The workshop of character is everyday life.
The uneventful and commonplace hour
is where the battle is lost or won.

MALTBIE D. BABCOCK

Character cannot be developed in ease and quiet.
Only through experience of trial and suffering
can the soul be strengthened, vision cleared,
ambition inspired, and success achieved.

HELEN KELLER

It is not the still calm of life, or in the repose
of a specific situation, that great characters are formed.

ABIGAIL ADAMS

The LORD has told you what is good,
and this is what he requires of you:
to do what is right, to love mercy,
and to walk humbly with your God.

MICAH 6:8 NLT

Courage is what it takes to stand up and speak;
courage is also what it takes to sit down and listen.

SIR WINSTON CHURCHILL

A Unique Song to Sing

....

What we have done for ourselves alone dies
with us; what we have done for others and
the world remains and is immortal.

ALBERT PIKE

We find our greatest joy, not in getting,
but in expressing what we are. We do not really live
for honors or for pay; our gladness is not
in the taking and holding, but in the doing,
the striving, the building, the living.
It is a higher joy to teach than to be taught.
It is good to get justice, but better to do it;
fun to have things, but more to make them.
The happy person is the one who lives the life of love,
not for the honors it may bring, but for the life itself.

R. J. BAUGHAN

You have a unique message to deliver,
a unique song to sing, a unique act of love to bestow.
This message, this song, and this act of love
have been entrusted exclusively to the one and only you.

JOHN POWELL

*D*o you want to stand out? Then step down.
Be a servant. If you puff yourself up, you'll get the wind
knocked out of you. But if you're content to simply
be yourself, your life will count for plenty.

MATTHEW 23:11–12 MSG

*W*hether sixty or sixteen, there is in every human being's
heart the love of wonder, the sweet amazement at the stars
and starlike things, the undaunted challenge of events,
the unfailing childlike appetite for what-next,
and the joy of the game of living.

SAMUEL ULLMAN

*N*othing important, or meaningful,
or beautiful, or interesting, or great ever came
out of imitations. The thing that is really hard,
and really amazing, is giving up on being perfect
and beginning the work of becoming yourself.

ANNA QUINDLEN

I pray thee, O God, that I may be beautiful within.

SOCRATES

It's in Christ that we find out who we are
and what we are living for. Long before we first heard
of Christ and got our hopes up, he had his eye on us,
had designs on us for glorious living, part of the overall
purpose he is working out in everything and everyone.

EPHESIANS 1:11-12 MSG

You have made us for Yourself, O Lord,
and our heart is restless until it rests in You.

ST. AUGUSTINE

$\mathcal{N}$o one ever attains very eminent success
by simply doing what is required of him;
it is the amount and excellence
of what is over and above the required
that determines the greatness of ultimate distinction.

CHARLES KENDALL ADAMS

$\mathcal{J}$esus just wants me to allow myself to be carved
into His image. The more I do, the more I realize
that I become more of myself...more of who
I authentically, truly, am. The more I surrender my life
to Jesus, the more I actually become me.

CHYNNA PHILLIPS

For in Him we live and move and have our being.

ACTS 17:28 NKJV

If you believe in God, it is not too difficult
to believe that He is concerned about the universe
and all the events on this earth. But the really staggering
message...is that this same God cares deeply about you
and your identity and the events of your life.

Count Your Blessings

I want to learn to live each moment and be
grateful for what it brings, asking no more.

GLORIA GAITHER

Counting your blessings is not something that necessarily happens in a moment, a day, or even a year. Sometimes the blessings that emerge from pain take an entire lifetime to reveal themselves, and that's a good thing. You never know when the challenge you are facing now will become an instant "Thank God" simply by virtue of not being as bad as what you've already survived.

In the end, I consider myself extremely lucky. At age nineteen, I paid tuition upfront in the "School of Adult Life." I learned about pain, anger, frustration, and perseverance. Without knowing those, I wouldn't fully recognize grace, victory, joy, beauty, peace, and gratitude. I thank God for all of it: I am still reaping the rewards of my Life Education. More importantly, I'm here to tell the story.

ELIZABETH BRYAN BRENNER

May your footsteps set you upon a lifetime journey of love. May you wake each day with His blessings and sleep each night in His keeping. And may you always walk in His tender care.

The LORD bless you, and keep you;
The LORD make His face shine on you,
And be gracious to you;
The LORD lift up His countenance on you,
And give you peace.

NUMBERS 6:24-26 NASB

Gratitude unlocks the fullness of life.
It turns what we have into enough, and more.
It turns denial into acceptance, chaos to order,
confusion to clarity.... It turns problems into gifts,
failures into successes,
the unexpected into perfect timing,
and mistakes into important events.
Gratitude makes sense of our past,
brings peace for today,
and creates a vision for tomorrow.

MELODY BEATTIE

Normal day, let me be aware of the treasure you are.
Let me learn from you, love you,
bless you before you depart. Let me not pass you by
in quest of some rare and perfect tomorrow.

Friendships, family ties, the companionship of little
children, an autumn forest flung in prodigality against
a deep blue sky, the intricate design and haunting fragrance
of a flower, the counterpoint of a Bach fugue or the melodic
line of a Beethoven sonata, the fluted note of bird song,
the glowing glory of a sunset: the world is aflame
with things of eternal moment.

E. MARGARET CLARKSON

$\mathcal{F}$rom the fullness of His grace we have
all received one blessing after another.

JOHN 1:16 NIV

$\mathcal{G}$ratitude...is not something we do at all.
Rather, it is a medium of grace, a gift of God
that softens the heart and enables it
to see and hear and receive
the things that come to it from God.

ROBERTA BONDI

Count your blessings.
Learn not to take benefits,
endowments, and pleasures for granted....
Thank God for them all.

J. I. PACKER

Oh, taste and see that the LORD is good;
Blessed is the man who trusts in Him!

PSALM 34:8 NKJV

Your Significance

....

God loves us for ourselves.
He values our love more than He values
galaxies of newly created worlds.

A. W. TOZER

$\mathcal{A}$ speaker started a seminar by holding up a twenty-dollar bill. The speaker asked, "Who would like this twenty-dollar bill?" Hands shot up all around the room. The speaker said, "I am going to give this twenty-dollar bill to one of you, but first let me do this." He crumpled up the twenty-dollar bill and dropped it on the ground, grinding it into the floor with his heel. He picked it up, crumpled and dirty, and asked, "Now who wants it?" Hands still went up all over the room. No matter what was done to the money, it was still desirable because it did not decrease in value.

Many times in life, you will be dropped, crumpled, or ground into the dirt by the circumstances that come your way and the decisions you make. You may feel as though you are worthless and useless. But you will never lose your value. Dirty or clean, crumpled or finely creased, you are still priceless to those who love you and to the One who made you.

*N*ot a single sparrow can fall to the ground
without your Father knowing it.
And the very hairs on your head are all numbered.
So don't be afraid; you are more valuable
to God than a whole flock of sparrows.

MATTHEW 10:29-31 NLT

*T*he value of a person is not measured
on an applause meter; it is measured
in the heart and mind of God.... Rest assured,
for on God's scale, the needle always reads high.

JOHN FISCHER

Our hunger for significance is a signal of who
we are and why we are here, and it also is the basis
of humanity's enduring response to Jesus.
For He always takes individual human beings
as seriously as their shredded dignity demands,
and He has the resources to carry through
with His high estimate of them.

DALLAS WILLARD

God made my life complete
when I placed all the pieces before Him....
God rewrote the text of my life when
I opened the book of my heart to His eyes.

PSALM 18:20, 24 MSG

I believe that nothing that happens to me
is meaningless, and that it is good
for us all that it should be so,
even if it runs counter to our own wishes.
As I see it, I'm here for some purpose,
and I only hope I may fulfill it.

DIETRICH BONHOEFFER

A human life is like a single letter
of the alphabet. It can be meaningless.
Or it can be a part of a great meaning.

Whether sixty or sixteen,
there is in every human being's heart
the love of wonder, the sweet amazement
at the stars and starlike things,
the undaunted challenge of events,
the unfailing childlike appetite for what-next,
and the joy of the game of living.

SAMUEL ULLMAN

So God created human beings in his own image;
In the image of God he created them.

GENESIS 1:27 NLT

Something to Count On

There stands, behind all that changes
and can change, only one unchangeable joy.
That is God.

HANNAH WHITALL SMITH

When we cry out with every fiber of our being,
"My soul thirsts for God, for the living God," then,
in time, there comes a seeing that is beyond sight.
We begin to see a spiritual reality that others do not see.
And we trust in that reality, betting our lives on it.
This is what the Bible means by faith. Faith involves
an entering into the knowledge of the invisible,
spiritual world and a living on the basis of that knowledge.

RICHARD J. FOSTER

What gives me hope is knowing God's character,
knowing what He's like...and that He doesn't change.
Therefore, no matter what changes in my life,
no matter what the circumstances are,
I don't have to lose hope, because I'm not trusting
in my life, I'm trusting in the One who holds my life: God.

LISA WHELCHEL

𝒩othing we can do will make God love us less;
nothing we do can make Him love us more.
He loves us unconditionally with an everlasting love.
All He asks of us is that we respond
to Him with the free will that He has given to us.

NANCIE CARMICHAEL

𝓜y God is changeless in his love for me
and he will come and help me.

PSALM 59:10 TLB

$\mathcal{W}$e are always in the presence of God....
There is never a nonsacred moment! His presence never
diminishes. Our awareness of His presence may falter,
but the reality of His presence never changes.

MAX LUCADO

$\mathcal{P}$erhaps this moment is unclear, but let it be—
even if the next, and many moments after that, are unclear,
let them be. Trust that God will help you work them out,
and that all the unclear moments will bring you
to that moment of clarity and action when you are known
by Him and know Him. These are the better
and brighter moments of His blessing.

Your love, O Lord, reaches to the heavens,
your faithfulness to the skies....
How priceless is your unfailing love!
Both high and low among men
find refuge in the shadow of your wings....
You give them drink from your river of delights.
For with you is the fountain of life;
in your light we see light.

PSALM 36:5, 7-9 NIV

The beauty of the earth, the beauty of the sky, the order
of the stars, the sun, the moon...their very loveliness is their
confession of God: for who made these lovely mutable
things, but He who is Himself unchangeable beauty?

ST. AUGUSTINE

What makes life worthwhile is having a big enough objective, something which catches our imagination and lays hold of our allegiance…. What higher, more exalted, and more compelling goal can there be than to know God?

J. I. PACKER

Show Your marvelous lovingkindness….
Keep me as the apple of Your eye;
Hide me under the shadow of Your wings.

PSALM 17:7-8 NKJV

Guideposts
on the Path

All the things in this world are gifts
and signs of God's love to us.
The whole world is a love letter from God.

PETER KREEFT

To be glad of life, because it gives you the chance to love
and to work and to play and to look up at the stars;
to be satisfied with your possessions, but not contented
with yourself until you have made the best of them...
to think seldom of your enemies, often of your friends,
and every day of Christ; and to spend as much time
as you can, with body and with spirit in God's out-of-doors—
these are little guideposts on the footpath to peace.

HENRY VAN DYKE

When we obey him, every path he guides us on
is fragrant with his loving-kindness and his truth.

PSALM 25:10 TLB

I am so renewed that all nature seems renewed around me and with me. The sky seems to be a purer, a cooler blue, the trees a deeper green, light is sharper on the outlines of the forest and the hills and the whole world is charged with the glory of God.

THOMAS MERTON

God's bright sunshine overhead,
God's flowers beside your feet...
And by such pleasant pathways led,
May all your life be sweet.

HELEN WAITHMAN

I love to think of nature
as an unlimited broadcasting station
through which God speaks to us every hour,
if only we will tune in.

GEORGE WASHINGTON CARVER

The LORD is my shepherd,
I shall not want.
He makes me lie down in green pastures;
He leads me beside quiet waters.
He restores my soul;
He guides me in the paths of righteousness
For His name's sake.

PSALM 23:1-3 NASB

If we are children of God,
we have a tremendous treasure in nature
and will realize that it is holy and sacred.
We will see God reaching out to us
in every wind that blows, every sunrise and sunset,
every cloud in the sky, every flower that blooms,
and every leaf that fades.

OSWALD CHAMBERS

Our Creator would never have made
such lovely days, and have given us the deep hearts
to enjoy them, above and beyond all thought,
unless we were meant to be immortal.

NATHANIEL HAWTHORNE

The huge dome of the sky is of all things sensuously
perceived the most like infinity. When God made space
and worlds that move in space, and clothed our world
with air, and gave us such eyes and such imaginations
as those we have, He knew what the sky would mean to us....
We cannot be certain that this was not indeed one
of the chief purposes for which Nature was created....
Because God created the Natural—invented it out
of His love and artistry—it demands our reverence.

C. S. LEWIS

I will teach you wisdom's ways
and lead you in straight paths.
When you walk, you won't be held back;
when you run, you won't stumble.
Take hold of my instructions; don't let them go.
Guard them, for they are the key to life.

PROVERBS 4:11-13 NLT

Always
Say a Prayer

God hears your prayers,
even the ones that aren't
fitting into words.

There's work to do, deadlines to meet;
You've got no time to spare,
But as you hurry and scurry
ASAP—Always Say A Prayer.

God knows how stressful life is;
He wants to ease our cares,
And He'll respond to all your needs
ASAP—Always Say A Prayer.

I call on you, O God, for you will answer me;
give ear to me and hear my prayer.

PSALM 17:6 NIV

Take the first step in faith. You don't have to see
the whole staircase, just take the first step.

MARTIN LUTHER KING JR.

There are four steps to accomplishment:
Plan Purposefully.
Prepare Prayerfully.
Proceed Positively.
Pursue Persistently.

Now faith is the substance of things hoped for,
the evidence of things not seen.

HEBREWS 11:1 NKJV

Do you believe that God is near? He wants you to.
He wants you to know that He is in the midst of your world.
Wherever you are as you read these words, He is present.
In your car. On the plane. In your office, your bedroom,
your den. He's near. And He is more than near. He is active.

MAX LUCADO

$\mathcal{M}$iracles happen to those who believe in them.

FRENCH PROVERB

$\mathcal{A}$lways stay connected to people
and seek out things that bring you joy.
Dream with abandon. Pray confidently.

BARBARA JOHNSON

$\mathcal{W}$hen you come to the edge of all the light you have,
and must take a step into the darkness of the unknown,
believe that one of two things will happen.
Either there will be something solid for you to stand on—
or you will be taught how to fly.

PATRICK OVERTON

Faith is to believe what we do not see; and the reward
of this faith is to see what we believe.

ST. AUGUSTINE

Do not pray for an easy life.
Pray to be a stronger person.
Do not pray for tasks equal to your powers.
Pray for powers equal to your tasks.
Then the doing of your work shall be no miracle,
but you shall be the miracle.

PHILLIPS BROOKS

The prayers we say shape the lives we live,
just as the lives we live shape the prayers we say.

TED LODER

Good people are not a perfect people;
good people are honest people,
faithful and unhesitatingly responsive
to the voice of God in their lives.
The more often they respond to that voice,
the easier it is to hear it the next time.

JOHN FISCHER

Anyone who does not believe in miracles is not a realist.

DAVID BEN-GURION

Steep yourself in God-reality, God-initiative,
God-provisions. You'll find all your everyday
human concerns will be met.
Don't be afraid of missing out.
You're My dearest friends!
The Father wants to give you the very kingdom itself.

LUKE 12:31-32 MSG

Make the World a Better Place

Do what you can to show
you care about other people,
and you will make our world a better place.

ROSALYNN CARTER

$\mathcal{E}$arly one morning, an old man was standing on the beach throwing starfish that had washed ashore in the night back out to sea. The man was weak and very old. Each throw took a little more energy out of him, but he kept on throwing.

The beach was so full of dying starfish that you could hardly take a step without finding another. A young man walking along the shoreline asked the old man what he was doing. He replied, "I'm making a difference."

The young man looked around and laughed. "A difference? There are thousands of starfish on this beach. You can't possibly think you will really make a difference."

The old man picked up another starfish and said, "It makes a difference to this one..." and threw it back into the sea.

For if you give, you will get! Your gift will return
to you in full and overflowing measure, pressed down,
shaken together to make room for more, and running over.
Whatever measure you use to give—large or small—
will be used to measure what is given back to you.

LUKE 6:38 TLB

It's easy to make a buck. It's tougher to make a difference....
You are educated. Your certification is in your degree.
You may think of it as the ticket to the good life.
Let me ask you to think of an alternative.
Think of it as your ticket to change the world.

TOM BROKAW

God loves me as God loves all people,
without qualification.... To be in the image of God
means that all of us are made for the purpose of knowing
and loving God and one another and of being loved in turn.

ROBERTA BONDI

One man gives freely, yet gains even more;
another withholds unduly, but comes to poverty.
A generous man will prosper;
he who refreshes others will himself be refreshed.

PROVERBS 11:24-25 NIV

$\mathcal{L}$ater in my career I finally appreciated the things that had lasting value and would impact society for generations to come. I noticed that most people who truly had a positive impact on people were others-centered and not self-centered.... People like Mother Teresa, President Lincoln... Martin Luther King Jr., Bill Wilson, and others, acted out of altruistic desires to better their generations and those to come. They made sacrifices and gave up relatively "cushy" lives in order to serve others and establish a legacy.... There is nothing inherently wrong in seeking success. At the same time, I wanted to ensure that my measure of success was something that would lead to significance, not necessarily in some earth-shattering invention or contribution, but something that would be others-centered and would serve to benefit others in society through God's power.

RICK BREKELBAUM

$\mathcal{G}$ive generously, for your gifts will return to you later.
Divide your gifts among many,
for in the days ahead you yourself may need much help.

ECCLESIASTES 11:1-2 TLB

$\mathcal{S}$ervice is the rent we each pay for living.
It is not something to do in your spare time;
it is the very purpose of life.

MARIAN WRIGHT EDELMAN

What Money Can't Buy

To feel rich, count all the things you have
that money can't buy.

$\mathcal{D}$uring my second year of nursing school our professor gave us a quiz. I breezed through the questions until I read the last one: "What is the first name of the woman who cleans the school?" Surely this was a joke. I had seen the cleaning woman several times, but how would I know her name? I handed in my paper, leaving the last question blank. Before the class ended, one student asked if the last question would count toward our grade. "Absolutely," the professor said. "In your careers, you will meet many people. All are significant. They deserve your attention and care, even if all you do is smile and say hello." I've never forgotten that lesson. I also learned her name was Dorothy.

JOANN C. JONES

A new command I give you: Love one another.
As I have loved you, so you must love one another.

JOHN 13:34 NIV

*G*ratitude is the heart of contentment.
I have never met a truly thankful,
appreciative person who was not profoundly happy.

NEIL CLARK WARREN

*F*irst it is necessary to stand on your own two feet.
But the minute you find yourself in that position,
the next thing you should do is reach
out your arms for a friend.

KRISTIN HUNTER LATTANY

It is said that for money you can have everything,
but you cannot. You can buy food, but not appetite;
medicine, but not health; knowledge,
but not wisdom; glitter, but not beauty;
fun, but not joy; acquaintances,
but not friends; servants, but not faithfulness;
leisure, but not peace.
You can have the husk of everything
for money, but not the kernel.

ARNE GARBORG

Contentment is not the fulfillment of what you want,
but the realization of how much you already have.

*L*et everything you say be good and helpful, so that your
words will be an encouragement to those who hear them.

EPHESIANS 4:29 NLT

*W*hen I get my own way, that's all I get.
I don't get the opportunity to deepen a relationship,
to love away the rough spots in a friend,
or to grow spiritually.

MARIANNE JONES

*A*t the end of your life you will never regret
not having passed one more test, not winning one more
verdict, or not closing one more deal. You will regret time
not spent with a spouse, a friend, a child, or a parent.

BARBARA BUSH

It's good to have money and the things
that money can buy, but it's good, too,
to check up once in a while and make sure
you haven't lost the things that money can't buy.

You're blessed when you're content
with just who you are—no more, no less.
That's the moment you find yourselves
proud owners of everything that can't be bought.

MATTHEW 5:5 MSG

Part of a Team

No matter what accomplishments
you achieve, somebody helps you.

ALTHEA GIBSON

A man was lost while driving through the countryside. As he tried to reach for the map, he accidentally drove into the ditch. Though he wasn't injured, his car was stuck deep in the mud. So the man walked to a nearby farm to ask for help.

"Warwick can get you out of that ditch," said the farmer, pointing to an old mule standing in a field. The man looked at the decrepit old mule and looked at the farmer, who just stood there repeating, "Yep, old Warwick can do the job."

The man figured he had nothing to lose. The two men and the mule made their way back to the ditch. The farmer hitched the mule to the car. With a snap of the reins, he shouted, "Pull, Fred! Pull, Jack! Pull, Ted! Pull, Warwick!" And the mule pulled the car right out of the ditch.

The man was amazed. He thanked the farmer, patted the mule, and asked, "Why did you call out all of those names before you called Warwick?" The farmer grinned and said, "Old Warwick is nearly blind. As long as he believes he's part of a team, he doesn't mind pulling."

May God, who gives this patience and encouragement,
help you live in complete harmony with each other.

ROMANS 15:5 NLT

When we dream alone it remains only a dream.
When we dream together, it is not just a dream.
It is the beginning of reality.

DOM HELDER CAMARA

Teamwork is the ability to work together toward
a common vision. The ability to direct
individual accomplishment toward
organizational objectives. It is the fuel that allows
common people to attain uncommon results.

ANDREW CARNEGIE

The greatest symbol of being different in show business
is pursuing excellence with integrity and showing grace
and mercy to coworkers and other people around you.
That means not getting as frantic as others who
are desperate for their movies to work. The Hollywood myth
is that you're only as good as your last project.
But these relationships are going to exist no matter
what movies I work on or what my next project is.

RALPH WINTER

*B*lessed are the peacemakers,
for they will be called children of God.

MATTHEW 5:9 NKJV

$\mathcal{C}$oming together is a beginning;
keeping together is progress;
working together is success.

$\mathcal{I}$t is a fact that in the right formation,
the lifting power of many wings can achieve twice
the distance of any bird flying alone.

$\mathcal{E}$ach of us has something different to contribute,
and no matter how small or insignificant it may seem,
it can be for the benefit of all.

LAURITZ MELCHIOR

Our job is not to straighten each other out,
but to help each other up.

NEVA COYLE

Since we have gifts that differ
according to the grace given to us,
each of us is to exercise them accordingly.

ROMANS 12:6 NASB

Hold Fast Your Dreams

Do not pray for dreams equal to your powers.
Pray for powers equal to your dreams.

ADELAIDE ANN PROCTER

Hold fast your dreams!
Within your heart
Keep one still, secret spot
Where dreams may go
And, sheltered so,
May thrive and grow
Where doubt and fear are not.
O keep a place apart,
Within your heart,
For little dreams to go!

LOUISE DRISCOLL

Hope deferred makes the heart sick,
but a dream fulfilled is a tree of life.

PROVERBS 13:12 NLT

The important thing is to strive towards a goal
which is not immediately visible.
That goal is not the concern of the mind, but of the spirit.

ANTOINE DE SAINT-EXUPÉRY

Some see things as they are and say, "Why?"
I dream things that never were and say, "Why not?"

This is your moment! Throw off the lines.
Leave behind the safe harbor.
Catch the wind and sail into the open waters.
Seek adventure. Go after your dreams.
Discover your life.

Reach high, for stars lie hidden in your soul.
Dream deep, for every dream precedes the goal.

PAMELA VAULL STARR

Go confidently in the direction of your dreams!
Live the life you've imagined.... You will meet
with a success unexpected in common hours.

HENRY DAVID THOREAU

*L*ife begins each morning....
Each morning is the open door to a new world—
new vistas, new aims, new tryings.

LEIGH MITCHELL HODGES

*N*o eye has seen, no ear has heard,
and no mind has imagined
what God has prepared
for those who love him.

1 CORINTHIANS 2:9 NLT

*I*t is necessary that we dream now and then.
No one ever achieved anything, from the smallest
to the greatest, unless the dream was dreamed first.

LAURA INGALLS WILDER

*T*he important thing really is not the deed well done
or the medal that you possess, but the dedication
and dreams out of which they grow.

ROBERT H. BENSON

If you have built castles in the air,
your work need not be lost; that is where they should be.
Now put the foundations under them.

HENRY DAVID THOREAU

May your dreams take you to the corners
of your smiles, to the highest of your hopes,
to the windows of your opportunities,
and to the most special places your heart has ever known.

Ambition is that grit in the soul
which creates disenchantment
with the ordinary and puts the dare into dreams.

MAX LUCADO

It's a thrill to fulfill your own childhood dreams,
but as you get older you may find that enabling
the dreams of others is even more fun.

RANDY PAUSCH

*F*or with God all things are possible.

MARK 10:27 NKJV

*L*et stars stand for those things which are ideal
and radiant in life; if we seek sincerely and strive
hard enough, it is not impossible to reach them,
even though the goals seem distant at the onset.
And how often do we touch stars when we find them
close by in the shining lives of great souls,
in the sparkling universe of humanity around us!

ESTHER BALDWIN YORK

A Life of Purpose

This is the true joy in life:
the being used for a purpose recognized
by yourself as a mighty one.

GEORGE BERNARD SHAW

If you want to know why you were placed on this planet, you must begin with God. You were born *by* His purpose and *for* His purpose.... How then do you discover the purpose you were created for?... The easiest way to discover the purpose of an invention is to ask the creator to explain it. The same method works for discovering your life's purpose. You can find what God, your creator, has revealed about life in His Word, the Bible. *Revelation* beats *speculation* any day.... There is a God who made you for a reason, and your life has profound meaning! We discover that meaning and purpose only when we make God the reference point of our lives.

RICK WARREN

The LORD will fulfill His purpose for me;
Your love, O LORD, endures forever—
do not abandon the works of Your hands.

PSALM 138:8 NIV

God has a purpose for your life
and no one else can take your place.

We need to set goals for ourselves. Start today....
If you don't have any goals, make your first goal
"getting some goals." You probably won't start living
happily ever after, but you may start living happily,
purposefully, and with gratitude.

MELODY BEATTIE

Aligning our life with God's purpose for us
gives a sense of destiny....
It gives form and direction to our life.

JEAN FLEMING

The highest excellence which an individual
can attain must be to work according to the best of his
genius and to work in harmony with God's creation.

J. H. SMYTH

My grace is sufficient for you,
for My strength is made perfect in weakness.

2 CORINTHIANS 12:9 NKJV

The purpose of life is a life of purpose.

ROBERT BYRNE

This is the real gift: we have been given the breath
of life, designed with a unique, one-of-a-kind soul
that exists forever—whether we live it as a burden
or a joy or with indifference doesn't change the fact
that we've been given the gift of *being* now and forever.
Priceless in value, we are handcrafted by God,
who has a personal design and plan for each of us.

Have a purpose in life, and having it,
throw into your work such strength of mind
and muscle as God has given you.

THOMAS CARLYLE

$\mathcal{L}$ife is so full
of meaning and purpose,
so full of beauty
—beneath its covering—
that you will find earth
but cloaks your heaven.

FRÀ GIOVANNI GIOCONDO

To develop inner strength is a pursuit that takes time.
Try to balance your outer goals with your inner purpose,
and remember you may not be able
to do everything you think you want to do.

I will make my people strong with power from me!
They will go wherever they wish, and wherever they go
they will be under my personal care.

ZECHARIAH 10:12 TLB

Do All the Good You Can

....

The difference between ordinary
and extraordinary is that little extra.

The good you do today,
people will often forget tomorrow;
Do good anyway.
Give the world the best you have,
and it may never be enough;
Give the world the best
you've got anyway....
You see, in the final analysis,
it is between you and God;
it was never between you
and them anyway.

MOTHER TERESA

Let us not become weary in doing good,
for at the proper time we will reap a harvest
if we do not give up. Therefore, as we have opportunity,
let us do good to all people.

GALATIANS 6:9-10 NIV

*N*ever let what you cannot do
interfere with what you can do.

*T*he reflective life is a way of living that prepares
the heart so that something of eternal significance
can be planted there. Who knows what seeds
may come to us, or what harvest will come of them.

KEN GIRE

*G*od has a history of using the insignificant
to accomplish the impossible.

RICHARD EXLEY

We give thanks to God always for all of you,
making mention of you in our prayers;
constantly bearing in mind your work of faith
and labor of love and steadfastness of hope.

1 THESSALONIANS 1:2-3 NASB

Our world is hungry for genuinely changed people.
Leo Tolstoy observed, "Everybody thinks of changing
humanity and nobody thinks of changing himself."
Let us be among those who believe
that the inner transformation of our lives
is a goal worthy of our best effort.

RICHARD J. FOSTER

The best kind of pride is that which compels
a person to do their best work—
even when no one is looking.

Do all the good you can by all the means you can
in all the ways you can in all the places you can
to all the people you can as long as ever you can.

JOHN WESLEY

Day by day the Lord also pours out his steadfast love
upon me, and through the night I sing his songs
and pray to God who gives me life.

PSALM 42:8 TLB

$\mathcal{E}$ven one day is a donation to eternity
and every hour is a contribution to the future.

Try to make each day reach as nearly as possible
the high-water mark of pure, unselfish, useful living.

BOOKER T. WASHINGTON

$\mathcal{W}$e must not, in trying to think about how
we can make a big difference, ignore the small daily
differences we can make which, over time,
add up to big differences that we often cannot foresee.

MARIAN WRIGHT EDELMAN

The Road Ahead

They are well guided that God guides.

SCOTTISH PROVERB

$\mathcal{M}$y Lord God, I have no idea where I am going.
I do not see the road ahead of me. I cannot know for certain
where it will end…. But I believe that the desire to please
You does in fact please You. And I hope I have that desire
in all that I am doing. I hope that I will never do anything
apart from that desire. And I know that if I do this,
You will lead me by the right road though I may know
nothing about it. Therefore will I trust You always,
though I may seem to be lost and in the shadow of death.
I will not fear, for You are ever with me.
And You will never leave me to face my perils alone.

THOMAS MERTON

$\mathcal{I}$ would rather walk with God in the dark
than go alone in the light.

MARY GARDINER BRAINARD

You are a chosen people, a royal priesthood,
a holy nation, a people belonging to God,
that you may declare the praises of him who
called you out of darkness into his wonderful light.

1 PETER 2:9 NIV

Heaven often seems distant and unknown,
but if He who made the road...is our guide,
we need not fear to lose the way.

HENRY VAN DYKE

I am always with you; you hold me by my right hand.

PSALM 73:23 NIV

The Lord directs the steps of the godly.
He delights in every detail of their lives.
Though they stumble, they will never fall,
for the Lord holds them by the hand.

PSALM 37:23-24 NLT

God, who has led you safely on so far,
will lead you on to the end.
Be altogether at rest in the loving holy confidence
which you ought to have in His heavenly providence.

FRANCIS DE SALES

We may not all reach God's ideal for us,
but with His help we may move in that direction
day by day as we relate every detail of our lives to Him.

God's Word acts as a light for our paths.
It can help scare off unwanted thoughts
in our minds and protect us from the enemy.

GARY SMALLEY AND JOHN TRENT

The very steps we take come from GOD;
otherwise how would we know where we're going?

PROVERBS 20:24 MSG

Whoever walks toward God one step,
God runs toward him two.

JEWISH PROVERB

Your word is a lamp to my feet
and a light for my path.

PSALM 119:105 NIV

Dreams and Goals

There is nothing like a dream
to create the future.

VICTOR HUGO

$\mathcal{A}$ dream becomes a goal when action
is taken toward its achievement.

BO BENNETT

$\mathcal{D}$ear brothers and sisters, I have not achieved it,
but I focus on this one thing: Forgetting the past
and looking forward to what lies ahead, I press on to reach
the end of the race and receive the heavenly prize
for which God, through Christ Jesus, is calling us.

PHILIPPIANS 3:13-14 NLT

$\mathcal{S}$hoot for the moon. Even if you miss,
you'll land among the stars.

LES BROWN

*N*othing is as real as a dream. The world can change around you, but your dream will not. Responsibilities need not erase it. Duties need not obscure it. Because the dream is within you, no one can take it away.

TOM CLANCY

*T*oss your faded dreams not into a trash bin but into a drawer where you are likely to rummage some bright morning.

ROBERT BRAULT

*E*very good and perfect gift is from above, coming down from the Father of the heavenly lights, who does not change like shifting shadows.

JAMES 1:17 NIV

$\mathcal{A}$ #2 pencil and a dream can take you anywhere.

JOYCE MEYER

$\mathcal{O}$h, how sweet the light of day, and how wonderful
to live in the sunshine! Even if you live a long time,
don't take a single day for granted.
Take delight in each light-filled hour.

ECCLESIASTES 11:7-8 MSG

The victory of success is half won when one gains the habit
of setting goals and achieving them. Even the most tedious
chore will become endurable as you parade through each
day convinced that every task, no matter how menial
or boring, brings you closer to fulfilling your dreams.

OG MANDINO

God can do anything, you know—
far more than you could ever imagine
or guess or request in your wildest dreams!

EPHESIANS 3:20 MSG

There is surely a future hope for you,
and your hope will not be cut off.

PROVERBS 23:18 NIV

Somehow I can't believe that there are any heights
that can't be scaled by a person who knows the secrets
of making dreams come true. This special secret...
can be summarized in four Cs. They are curiosity,
confidence, courage, and constancy.

WALT DISNEY

One hundred years from today
your present income will be inconsequential.
One hundred years from now it won't matter
if you got that big break, took the trip to Europe,
or finally traded up to a Mercedes....
It will matter that you knew God.

DAVID SIBLEY

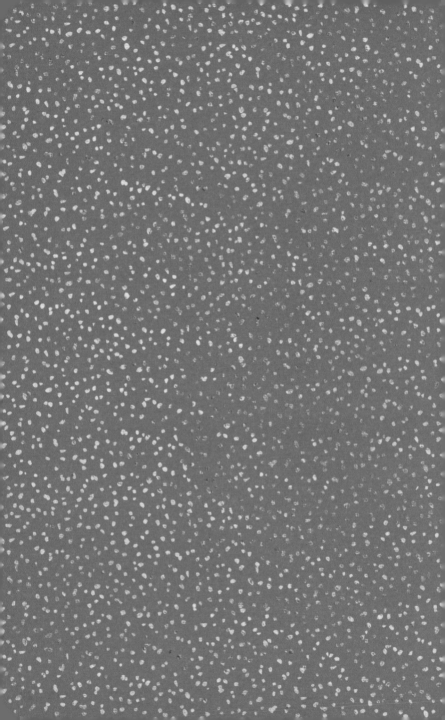